Dutch in Michigan

DISCOVERING THE PEOPLES OF MICHIGAN
Arthur W. Helweg and Linwood H. Cousins, Series Editors

Ethnicity in Michigan: Issues and People
Jack Glazier, Arthur W. Helweg

French Canadians in Michigan
John P. DuLong

African Americans in Michigan
Lewis Walker, Benjamin C. Wilson, Linwood H. Cousins

Albanians in Michigan
Frances Trix

Jews in Michigan
Judith Levin Cantor

Amish in Michigan
Gertrude Enders Huntington

Italians in Michigan
Russell M. Magnaghi

Germans in Michigan
Jeremy W. Kilar

Poles in Michigan
Dennis Badaczewski

Dutch in Michigan
Larry ten Harmsel

Asian Indians in Michigan
Arthur W. Helweg

Discovering the Peoples of Michigan is a series of publications examining the state's rich multicultural heritage. The series makes available an interesting, affordable, and varied collection of books that enables students and lay readers to explore Michigan's ethnic dynamics. A knowledge of the state's rapidly changing multicultural history has far-reaching implications for human relations, education, public policy, and planning. We believe that Discovering the Peoples of Michigan will enhance understanding of the unique contributions that diverse and often unrecognized communities have made to Michigan's history and culture.

Dutch in Michigan

Larry ten Harmsel

Michigan State University Press

East Lansing

Copyright © 2002 by Larry ten Harmsel

∞ The paper used in this publication meets the minimum requirements
of ANSI/NISO Z39.48-1992 (R 1997) (Permanence of Paper)

Michigan State University Press
East Lansing, Michigan 48823-5202

Printed and bound in the United States of America

08 07 06 05 04 03 02   1 2 3 4 5 6 7 8 9 10

LIBRARY OF CONGRESS CATALOGING-IN-PUBLICATION DATA
Ten Harmsel, Larry, 1945–
Dutch in Michigan / Larry ten Harmsel.
p. cm. — (Discovering the peoples of Michigan)
Includes bibliographical references and index.
ISBN 0-87013-620-8 (pbk. : alk. paper)
1. Dutch Americans—Michigan—History. 2.
Immigrants—Michigan—History. 3. Michigan—History. 4.
Michigan—Ethnic relations. I. Title. II. Series.
F575.D9 T46 2002
977.4'0043931—dc21
2002003485

Discovering the Peoples of Michigan. The editors wish
to thank the Kellogg Foundation for their generous support.

Cover design by Ariana Grabec-Dingman
Book design by Sharp Des!gns, Inc.

COVER PHOTO: Lumbermen wearing Dutch *boerenhoeden* (farmer's caps) hauling logs with
teams of horses. Courtesy of the Hope College Collection of the Joint Archives of Holland.

Visit Michigan State University Press on the World Wide Web at:
www.msupress.msu.edu

In memory of my grandparents

Anna Hansum Disselkoen (1901–1978)
Anthony Disselkoen (1896–1973)
Johanna Krommendijk ten Harmsel (1889–1955)
Hermanus ten Harmsel (1885–1975)

They found the promised land in Michigan.

SERIES ACKNOWLEDGMENTS

Discovering the Peoples of Michigan is a series of publications that resulted from the cooperation and effort of many individuals. The people recognized here are not a complete representation, for the list of contributors is too numerous to mention. However, credit must be given to Jeffrey Bonevich, who worked tirelessly with me on contacting people as well as researching and organizing material.

The initial idea for this project came from Mary Erwin, but I must thank Fred Bohm, director of the Michigan State University Press, for seeing the need for this project, for giving it his strong support, and for making publication possible. Also, the tireless efforts of Keith Widder and Elizabeth Demers, senior editors at Michigan State University Press were vital in bringing this project to fruition. Keith put his heart and soul into this series, and his dedication was instrumental in its success.

Otto Feinstein and Germaine Strobel of the Michigan Ethnic Heritage Studies Center patiently and willingly provided names for contributors and constantly gave this project their tireless support.

My late wife, Usha Mehta Helweg, was the initial editor. She meticulously went over manuscripts. Her suggestions and advice were crucial. Initial typing, editing, and formatting were also done by Majda Seuss, Priya Helweg, and Carol Nickolai.

Many of the maps in the series were drawn by Fritz Seegers while the graphics showing ethnic residential patterns in Michigan were done by the Geographical Information Center (GIS) at Western Michigan University under the directorship of David Dickason. Additional maps have been contributed by Ellen White.

Russell Magnaghi must also be given special recognition for his willingness to do much more than be a contributor. He provided author contacts as well as information to the series' writers. Other authors and organizations provided comments on other aspects of the work. There are many people that were interviewed by the various authors who will remain anonymous. However, they have enabled the story of their group to be told. Unfortunately, their names are not available, but we are grateful for their cooperation.

Most of all, this work is a tribute to the writers who patiently gave their time to write and share their research findings. Their contributions are noted and appreciated. To them goes most of the gratitude.

ARTHUR W. HELWEG, *Series Co-editor*

Contents

Background 1
Seceders 3
A Meager Paradise 6
Heresy and Sins 10
   Traditional Saying 10
The Civil War to World War I 15
   Hendrik Meijer 16
Into the Modern Age 19
   Joke 22
Provisional Conclusions 23
   Hollywood in West Michigan 25
   Common Dutch Words 27

Dutch Recipes 29
Louis Padnos 31
Logging 35

Notes 39
For Further Reference 43
Index 47

The Dutch in Michigan

Background

Compared to other European countries, the Netherlands did not see many of its inhabitants go to the United States as immigrants. The nation had a reputation for social and economic stability, as well as a long history of tolerance. In the century of great European immigration, when entire regions of countries such as Ireland were depopulated, the proportion of Hollanders to join the tide never amounted to as much as 1 percent of the population, although the land is small and very densely populated. "The proverbial Dutch attachment to family, faith, and fatherland outweighed the appeal of overseas utopias."[1]

Although New York City was once called New Amsterdam, and Hollanders left traces of their culture all along the banks of the Hudson River, they came to America only in small numbers. Between 1776 and 1845, there were fewer than one hundred Dutch immigrants a year. By 2001 a total of fewer than three hundred thousand Dutch immigrants to the United States had been recorded, compared to more than a million each from the smaller nations of Sweden and Denmark and far greater numbers from Germany, England, Ireland, and Italy.

In the mid-nineteenth century, however, from 1847 to 1857, more than a thousand people a year arrived from Holland. They settled in farming communities and towns throughout west Michigan and in a few other parts of the United States and established cultural institutions that continued to welcome new immigrants for more than a century. These new arrivals were mostly Calvinists, members of a group that had seceded from the state church (also Calvinist) of the Dutch government. To understand their situation, it is necessary to outline a bit of their history in the Netherlands.

The Dutch government, reacting to rationalist influences and a new monarchy in the years after Waterloo (1815) had changed the way the state church was run.

William I (1815 – 40) had appointed influential government figures to the Synod, a centralized ruling body, thus diminishing the autonomy of local congregations, which then held proportionately fewer seats. This Synod had changed the songbooks used during worship by adding hymns that struck many people as being less holy than their traditional Psalms, which were taken from the Genevan Psalter. The government was, in effect, trying to bring itself into the modern age. William I hoped to dismantle some of the ancient laws and practices encouraging states to torment and persecute people on account of their religion. Most galling to the Seceders, he had tinkered with the doctrines of historic Calvinism, especially the Belgic Confessions. The Belgic Confessions, technically affirmed by the Dutch state, called on the government to stamp out heresies, singling out Catholicism and Anabaptist teachings for particular hellfire and brimstone. The Church, in effect, had become an embarrassment to the crown (and vice versa, as far as the Seceders were concerned). What the Seceders wanted, it seems, was the power and influence accorded them by an official State religion without the intrusion of the government into churchly matters. They soon found they could not have it both ways.

For a time in the 1830s, turning the tables on the would-be persecutors, the government imposed a regimen of fines, harassment, and imprisonment on those Seceders who protested too loudly. By 1840, however, under a new set of religious laws and a new king, the harsh treatment had largely disappeared. Yet the Seceders' disaffection with the Netherlands continued to build. Eventually it would lead them to Michigan.

Seceders

The image of the Netherlands as a prosperous, open-minded, humane, and stodgily progressive nation has persisted from the Golden Age to the present. This brief spate of official persecution was very much out of character in a land where since the Age of Erasmus (a Catholic humanist), Spinoza (a secular Portuguese Jew), and Rembrandt (an Anabaptist), people of widely divergent ideas had lived together peacefully. Much of the Seceders' resentment was aimed at the equal treatment the government had guaranteed to Catholics, Baptists, and Jews, who were accorded state support for their religious and educational activities and enjoyed social and legal rights often lacking in other European nations. One could say that the people who led boatloads of Hollanders to Michigan were among the few American immigrants to flee a spirit of *tolerance* in their native land.

When a group of these Calvinists decided the time had come to leave their native land, they set forth the reasoning behind their decision in a small pamphlet called "Landverhuizing" (Emigration). This brief essay, published by Anthonie Brummelkamp and Albertus C. van Raalte in 1846, is a germinal document for understanding the group of people who, just a few months later, would set out for the dense forests and swampy lowlands of western Michigan.

Brummelkamp and van Raalte, brothers-in-law and Seceder pastors (the dissident group was called *Afgescheiden*—those who are cut off—in Dutch), had withdrawn themselves from the state church of the Netherlands several years earlier. Their conflicts with the official church were well known to their audience in the impoverished agricultural provinces of the Netherlands.

These ideological disputes, outlined previously, lie behind nearly everything Brummelkamp and van Raalte said in their essay. Yet the two men also stressed issues of bread and butter, which would have been more important to their working-class audience. People should have the right, they said, "working in peace, to eat the bread that they have earned by the sweat of their brow."[2] Especially in the aftermath of the potato blight, which had hit the Netherlands with demoralizing thoroughness in the summer of 1845, this was a compelling reason for considering emigration. Many rural Hollanders had seen their entire potato crop destroyed, and, with the blight still raging in the summer of 1846, there was little hope for a quick recovery. Complicating the farmers' plight were a profound change in European economies; a high rate of taxation; and an outmoded, fragmented national infrastructure.

The port cities of Amsterdam and Rotterdam dominated the nation's economy. The outlying provinces did not keep pace with market requirements and found themselves increasingly isolated from the centers of activity. For many farmers, life was becoming difficult, sometimes desperate. Even those who could avoid poverty were worried about the future. Prospects for their children were bleak, not only because of the financial uncertainties of the times but also because of the additional burden of overpopulation—the third issue addressed by Brummelkamp and van Raalte.

Choosing their words carefully, to make clear that they were not accusing God of bad management, the authors of "Emigration to the United States" insisted that the problem was not overpopulation as such (since mankind had been commanded in the book of Genesis to "be fruitful and multiply"), but the massing of too many people in too small a place. They cited the biblical story of the tower of Babel, and suggested that the Netherlands was becoming such a place. "People must spread out," they argued; "It is the will of God; then life will be better both for those who stay and for those who leave."[3]

Despite their dire assessment of the Netherlands as a religious oppressor, an economic mirage, and an incipient tower of Babel, however, Brummelkamp and van Raalte were not ready to give up on it. Much of their pamphlet was devoted to a last-ditch appeal for assistance. In an access of optimism, they asked the government to send the Seceders to Colonial Java, in the Dutch East Indies,

> where the air is healthier; where cool breezes blow; where plant life flourishes; where the forests teem with wild deer, cattle and wild pigs. In view of these favorable conditions it will be possible to devote all one's energies to God, energies which are now wasted as a result of the cares of the world."[4]

Figure 1. Main areas of Emigration from the Netherlands.

They insisted that they be granted land, housing allowances, and subsidies for churches and schools; in return they offered to become missionaries to the "25 million pagans" of Indonesia.

Not surprisingly, the government declined to provide the requested amenities. It should also come as no surprise that the Seceders made no serious missionary efforts among the American Indians who lived in west Michigan.

A Meager Paradise

Late in the summer of 1846, while Brummelkamp (who eventually abandoned the idea of emigrating) kept watch over his congregations in their native land, van Raalte led several hundred settlers to the United States. He intended to purchase land in Wisconsin, where Hollanders had already achieved a foothold. However, delays in traveling and an early winter forced him to stop in Detroit. There he had a chance encounter with Dutch Catholics on their way to Wisconsin and soon changed his mind about that state. Its Dutch population was dominated by Catholics, and a man who believed it was the duty of the central government to stamp out "idolatrous Papism" would not lead his people into such a place.

Casting about for other possibilities, he heard about available lands in western Michigan and was soon persuaded to explore the relatively uninhabited land around what is now Holland, Michigan, with the result that it became the center of Dutch immigration in the United States.

Van Raalte chose the land around Holland partly because of its isolation: that way he thought he could keep "foreign" influences on his flock at a minimum. The very difficulty of the place also appealed to him. It was thickly wooded, like most of the state. The low-lying terrain, much of it black dirt or muck left by a prehistoric river flowing through it prior to the last ice age, resembled the landscape in the Netherlands. A network of murky streams and rivers webbed its surface, carrying a rich load of silt toward Lake Michigan. There were only a few rolling hills in the territory van Raalte explored, rimmed by the sandy dunes of the lake to the west. Except for the virgin forests, it must have seemed like a primeval version of his homeland, which Napoleon had once called "some silt at the end of my principal rivers."

Although the Treaty of Chicago (1833) had displaced most Native Americans from this part of Michigan, there were a few Indians still living in the region. Aside from occasional clearings and oak openings, the land would require backbreaking efforts to be made suitable for farming. Existing farms were scarce and impoverished. Yet farming was the only way of life most of the van Raalte's followers knew, and it was the desire even of those who could not afford land in the Netherlands.

Despite what he knew to be great hurdles, van Raalte established in Holland, Michigan, a *kolonie* that, over the course of the next century, attracted thousands of Dutch immigrants. Their homeland comprised some thirteen thousand square miles, parcelled out among eleven million inhabitants. Eventually, these settlers and their offspring would acquire more than two thousand square miles of land in Michigan, an immense tract by Dutch standards.

Engbertus Van der Veen, arriving in August of 1847, found the place

dismal and fearful. . . . The moaning sounds of the western pine, the night birds' shrill, weird cries, the hoots of the owls, the squeaking of birds and croaks of the insects throughout the woods made a painful impression on us who had come from Amsterdam, and filled us with dismay."[5]

In the light of morning he saw his countrymen emerge from "their log shanties or from under branches of trees that they had piled against the trunks of fallen trees."[6] What the early settlers enjoyed was a meager paradise compared to Java. The winters were much colder than Dutch winters, the snow was deeper, and the winds whipping off the waters of Lake Michigan held a merciless chill. Still the people kept coming.

Between 1820 and 1840, the number of Hollanders coming to America had averaged fewer than one hundred a year. Between 1847 and 1857 ten times that number arrived, nearly half of whom made west Michigan their destination. Although such an increase was considerable, it had little effect on life in the Netherlands, except in those villages where Seceders predominated. Fewer than one in five of the immigrants came from the cities, the rest having lived in isolated rural provinces.

The newcomers worked at clearing acreage and planting crops. They had had no experience of lumbering in their homeland, and most had no idea how to fell a tree. For the first several years supplies had to be carried on foot from Grand Rapids or Allegan, more than twenty miles distant. Many died of disease and the harshness of winter.

The settlers who came to west Michigan were the exception rather than the rule for immigrants. They were not desperately poor. More than 65 percent of them were from the middle classes, although as many as one-fifth had sought public assistance from the Dutch government. They normally arrived in groups rather than as individuals. In some ways, however, they followed traditional patterns. They moved as part of an extended chain forged by family and church. They followed the folkways they had known back home, and, despite the strangeness of the new land, found much that was familiar to them. Many letters tell of meeting old neighbors or long-lost relatives from the Netherlands.

"I took a trip to the colony," said Marcus Nienhuis in 1854, in a letter back home, "and met a friend of yours. I saw the woman standing in her doorway and asked some directions. As soon as she opened her mouth, I could tell that she was from Drenthe and I asked if she was the wife of Harm Smidt. In surprise she answered, 'Yes.'"[7]

People continued to speak in their regional dialects, and formed villages that were virtual transplants from the rural provinces of the Netherlands. Within a few years of the first arrivals, the towns around Holland had sprouted Dutch names: Overisel, Drenthe, Vriesland, Staphorst, Harlem, and Groningen, among others. Sometimes as many as two hundred immigrants would arrive at once, putting a strain on the welcome that was extended to them. However, they kept coming. Shortly after the first settlement was established, the community's leaders hired an American to set up the first school in the area. Classes were taught in both Dutch and English, with the heaviest emphasis being on the new language. The settlers early recognized that in order to prosper they would need to learn the language of the country around them.

Being primarily agricultural people, or at least aspiring to that condition, the settlers utterly failed to comprehend the ways of the Indians they met, a loosely mixed group of Ottawas and Catholic Potawatomies, who were perceived by the settlers as both racially and religiously beyond the pale. Now and then a Hollander would find a deer hanging in a tree and take it home. More often the newcomers would gather up items the Indians had apparently abandoned in the woods, such as axes or troughs for making maple syrup, not knowing that the owners intended to return and use them the next year. Van Raalte, among his

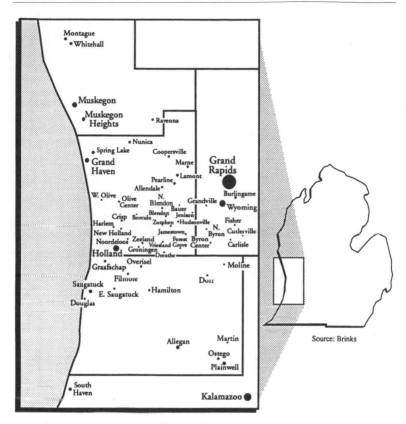

Figure 2. Dutch Settlements in West Michigan.

other duties as church father, oversaw the return of several thousand maple troughs, with negotiated settlements being reached for those items that had been lost or destroyed.[8]

Many of the original tracts of land were purchased from individual Indian landowners, and the settlers worked at maintaining good relations with them, despite misunderstandings. Yet the late 1840s was a time when the Indian presence in Michigan was diminishing. Most of the Potawatamies had been resettled outside the state, and the Ottawas were being pushed toward enclaves farther north. An outbreak of fevers, some of them malarial, in the summers of 1847 and 1848 speeded the process of Indian displacement. Some settlers saw God's will behind

> **A Traditional Saying**
>
> "Two Hollanders, a church; three Hollanders, a heresy."

the high rate of Indian mortality during these bouts of sickness; more likely, however, the cause was a combination of low resistance among the Native Americans and a folk remedy for fever that included sudden immersion in cold water—a treatment that occasionally killed the sufferer outright.[9]

New settlers kept arriving in a steady stream. Holland, the heart of the *kolonie*, with a population of about 1,500 in 1850, was spreading its influence through the surrounding villages, and had sent many young workers and families to urban satellite communities. The Dutch in Michigan, despite their hardships, were living out an American success story. Yet their sense of unity, which had given them strength in the early years, would not last for long.

Heresy and Sins

The religious difficulties of the Seceders, who later became the core of the settlement in Michigan—*de kolonie*, were of tremendous importance to those pastors who, like van Raalte, led their flocks into the wilderness in the late 1840s. Though religious disturbances did not cause the emigration, they contributed to its character and its troubles.

The Dutch had long been known for a proclivity to theological squabbling. "Is there a mongrel sect in Christendom," asked one seventeenth-century onlooker, "which does not croak and spawn and flourish in their Sooterkin bogs?" Another said,"They are so generally bred up to the Bible that almost every Cobbler is a Dutch doctor of divinity . . . yet fall those inward illuminations so different that sometimes seven religions are found in one family."[10] Religion did lend a special cast to the earliest settlement. Although fewer than 2 percent of the Dutch population belonged to this fringe religious group, Seceders accounted for almost 50 percent of the immigrants to America before

Figure 3. "Attention! The church council urgently requests that users of tobacco refrain from spitting or throwing down tobacco, which is not fitting in God's House." Source: Brinks.

1850. Even among these conservative folk, however, more than 90 percent listed economic reasons, rather than religion, as foremost among the causes for their move.

Whatever else they left behind in the old country when they came to the new community, however, these people took along their mastery of the art of schism, which would become increasingly obvious as the *kolonie* developed. The religious reasons for the migration, though they lay dormant in the consciousness of most immigrants, were to set the tone for much of their subsequent history. The opposing pressures of isolation and assimilation—those twin demons of every group wishng to define itself without losing all vestiges of an identity—began to assert themselves. The demons took a theological form.

Concerning secular issues, there was virtually no disagreement among the immigrants. A certain amount of assimilation was inevitable, and was welcomed. A commitment to a new country cannot be founded simply on disaffection with the old. The farmers worked to adopt current American agricultural practices, which sometimes differed from the Dutch ways, and their letters home showed genuine pride in their accomplishments.[11] The villages hired English-speaking teachers for both adults and children to ensure the removal of language barriers. Despite limited intercourse with nearby towns, the city of Holland soon adopted English as its primary language. By 1880 the town's English-language newspaper far outsold its Dutch counterpart, and by 1900 there was only one daily newspaper, the *Holland City News*.

By 1880, some ten thousand people in Michigan were Dutch-born, and the second generation numbered another thirty thousand. They had established themselves in urban enclaves—each corresponding to a village or province in their homeland—in Grand Rapids, Muskegon, Grand Haven, and Kalamazoo.[12]

They established working relationships with "Yankee" merchants in nearby cities. They showed a uniquely northern American sentiment on the issue of slavery, going so far in 1855 as to request "humbly and kindly" that a group of southern churches founded by Dutch American slaveholders be kept out of their religious fellowship.[13] When the Civil War began, just thirteen years after the founding of the community, more than four hundred of their young men fought for the Union. These people were dedicated to the idea of becoming Americans—not merely Hollanders on foreign soil—and of making contributions to the life of their new nation. R. T. Kuiper expressed his feelings in a letter to his homeland.

Life is more roomy here, freer, easier, more common; there is more open-heartedness. . . . There are far fewer formalities and rules of conduct.

> Everyone associates on a more equal level. True, everyone is called "mis-
> ter," but no one "sir," with the exception of the preacher, who is still
> addressed as "Dominie." But no one removes his hat for him. . . .[14]

In secular terms, then, they assimilated quite successfully.

However, in religious terms their attempts at assimilation met with
shattering opposition. Upon their formation, the churches of the
Holland settlement had begun the process of affiliating themselves
with the Dutch Reformed Church in America (later the Reformed
Church in America, the RCA), a denomination with a history going back
to the era of Peter Stuyvesant, the seventeenth-century leader of New
Amsterdam, later New York. Over the years it had, in the estimation of
the settlers, become quite Americanized. Instead of serving as another
strand in a developing social network, then, membership in the RCA
became the catalyst for a rupture. The process can be seen in the
Minutes of Classis Holland, a unique record of church affairs in the first
ten years of the settlement.

This classis, the governing council of the immigrant church, concerned itself with an array of matters extending well beyond church
polity, including private land ownership, travel expenses for new arrivals,
the disposal of bad debts, sexual misconduct, the clearing of land, boat-
building, and dozens of other primarily secular issues. The church was,
in effect, the entire government; its influence was felt in every area of the
settlers' lives. Such an extended role was common to churches in new
communities across America, as they provided a sense of solidity,
confidence, and continuity otherwise missing in a trackless wilderness.

However, religious factions arose among the dozen or so villages in
Classis Holland. The minutes hint at whispered charges of heresy. On 15
May 1853, the Church of Drenthe presented a Certificate of Secession to
the Classis containing one brief sentence: "We discontinue fellowship
with you, because we no longer can nor may be in fellowship with
you."[15] The reasons for this new secession were vaguely lumped
together by the dissenters under the term "worldliness," a word whose
specific meaning could change but whose emotional content was clear:
there was a threat to identity, a fear of being lost in the American melting pot. By 1857 the crisis had erupted in a schism. One-third of the

Dutch community broke loose from the RCA, sundering families, congregations, and villages. They declared themselves eternally opposed to the "church-destroying heresy and sins which are among you."[16] The dissidents created the Christian Reformed Church (CRC). They made the claim of all dissident groups around the world: they were returning to the "true roots" of their organization. Instead of joining the American Synod of the RCA, these churches allied themselves with a similar religious movement in the Netherlands, renewing ties that had not, in any case, been long broken.

A pattern of disagreement and competition between the RCA and the CRC soon arose, which, although civilized and toned down as the twenty-first century began, has been reflected in the community ever since. Early on, this rift had all the marks of a family spat. The "church-destroying heresy" alluded to in the articles of secession consisted of little more than a tendency on the part of the RCA to allow members to join Masonic lodges and the rumor of an episode in which several non-Calvinist church leaders had been allowed to share in Holy Communion. Yet those were simply symptoms of a general decline in holiness to frontier Puritans. One opponent of the split claimed that the dissenters were in "opposition to hymns, to funeral services, to dead bodies in church during a funeral, to flowers on caskets, to church organs, to fire insurance, to lightning rods, to flowers on bonnets, to white dresses, to the English language, to Christmas trees, to vaccination, and to picnics."[17]

Later scandals and splits involved issues even more obscure. As with most family quarrels, such debates reinforced rather than diminished a sense of ethnic solidarity; they left outsiders mystified about the hidden motivations of these curious Dutchmen. By the time of the Civil War, it was becoming apparent that the religious conflict concerned not theology but strategies of integration with the modern world. What the immigrants engaged in was not so much a war between opposites (which is how they saw it) as a disagreement over tactics. One group (the RCA) wished to effect a rather significant level of assimilation, while the other (the CRC) emphasized the need to retain moral purity in the face of an immoral modern onslaught. Particular issues were little more than pawns in a larger game.[18]

The Civil War to World War I

In 1862, while the Civil War dragged on with no end in sight, Albertus van Raalte was trying to patch together his segment of the Dutch *kolonie*. That year he wrote his son Dirk, serving with Company I of Michigan's 25th Regiment, to ask for money. The elder van Raalte was raising funds for an academy in Holland (he had donated the land) and apparently hoped that a gift from his fighting son would serve a symbolic purpose in launching what was to become Hope College and in drawing his fragmented people together. The rapid growth and diversification of the community meant that by the 1860s there were many small towns and many local leaders. By campaigning to start a college, van Raalte was also angling to maintain his personal status as the first among them.

His son Dirk was not an easy touch:

> I won't give one red cent. . . . It would be better if the students came here carrying a rifle and a knapsack on their backs. They are needed here. . . . We have to bleed and die for our country, while they remain at home living off us—and then make sport of us too.[19]

The years between the end of the Civil War and the beginning of World War I saw steady growth and development in the twin Dutch subcultures, which remained separate though they lived side by side. Their numbers were replenished by successive waves of new immigrants from the Netherlands, swelling when the American economy was good and waning when there was a depression or panic. New arrivals continued to come from the sand provinces of Overijssel, Gelderland, and Drenthe, but now they were outnumbered by settlers from the clay-soil provinces of Friesland, Groningen, and Zeeland. These infusions of newcomers kept a sense of Netherlandic provincial culture alive, when the second and sometimes third generations of Dutch Americans might otherwise have assimilated into the mainstream culture more readily.

In the 1880s, when the number of emigrants leaving for America had more than doubled from its levels in the 1840s and 1850s, the young

Hendrik Meijer

In 1908 Hendrik Meijer—at that time working in a foundry and not yet speaking much English—played clarinet in the Holland, Michigan, community band. One of their performances began with a prayer. "It was all in English, and all of a sudden everyone had their eyes closed," he wrote. "So I amused myself by looking out to see what was going on in the street. They are dumb people as far as that goes . . . way behind the Netherlands. If you say 'I don't believe in anything,' they just look at you. One man said . . . 'not to believe— that's awful.' Of course, I told him why I didn't believe, but then they come up with all those Bible verses. Always talking about Christianity and Christ, but they don't practice what they preach."[20]

Vincent Van Gogh depicted the plight of poor workers and farmers, whom he called "The Potato Eaters," in a haunting series of paintings and drawings. These impoverished countrymen were a symbol of something gone terribly wrong with the nation's life, a sort of rebuke for the difficulties of the industrial age. Even at its most intense, however, the emigration was not widespread. A scant 12 percent of townships in the Netherlands, all of them agricultural, contributed three-quarters of the total number, which averaged slightly more than two thousand people a year. As in years past, a sizeable majority (80 percent) of the immigrants described themselves as farmers or farm workers.

By the turn of the twentieth century, however, farmland in Michigan had become expensive. Furthermore, Dutch neighborhoods in cities like Grand Rapids (where they comprised 40 percent of the population) provided an attractive alternative to farm life together with opportunities for industrial employment. Consequently, most of the later immigrants moved into the cities, where they were likely to see familiar faces from the villages and churches they had left behind.

There was also a new kind of immigrant arriving: the radicalized and displaced industrial worker. Since such people were generally unattached young men, unlikely to attend church or get involved in mainstream social activities, not much record exists of their experi-

Figure 4. Ninth Street Christian Reformed Church. Courtesy of the Hope College Collection of the Joint Archives of Holland.

ence. Hendrik Meijer, a young laborer from Hengelo in the province of Overijssel, was a follower of the Dutch utopian anarchist Domela Nieuwenhuis.

In 1907 he wrote to his fiancée about a meeting with some acquaintances in Holland, Michigan:

> We had a long discussion about total abstinence. I was supported by three people from Zaandam and one Amsterdamer; all four were anarchists. We decided to form a group. We were asked to distribute brochures among the Hollanders. People need it here, because they are all hypocrites.[21]

This cell of teetotaler socialists never attracted more than a few dozen members in the conservative communities of west Michigan.

Meijer eventually moved to Greenville, where a Danish settlement flourished. Thirty years later, no longer an anarchist, he began a grocery business that eventually became the chain of hypermarkets still bearing his name.

During the first three decades of the twentieth century, the Dutch communities in Michigan gained an increasing economic and cultural self-sufficiency, creating or consolidating many of the institutions— hospitals, nursing homes, churches, and schools—that would help to transmit their sense of identity to subsequent generations. Because of the divided loyalties between the CRC and the RCA, which eventually came to be about the same size, many of their institutions developed in pairs. Even the smallest villages supported both a Reformed and a Christian Reformed Church; so also the community at large developed parallel systems of higher education. Hope College (founded in 1866) and Western Theological Seminary (founded in 1884), located in Holland, provided the Midwestern RCA with many of its church and community leaders. Drawing their faculties from a pool that included East Coast members of the RCA, Hope College and Western Theological Seminary both retained a modestly ethnic cast, but were much more Americanized than their counterpart in Grand Rapids. Calvin College and Seminary (founded in 1876), serving the CRC, drew heavily upon Dutch universities for its faculty, with the result that Calvin's character remained comparatively more Netherlandic for many years.

Members of the RCA typically sent their children to public schools, while the CRC encouraged its members to educate their children in private Christian schools. As a result, two excellent school systems developed side by side in west Michigan. A heady array of newspapers and magazines appeared during these years as well, many of them in Dutch. *De Hollander, De Stoompost, De Grondwet, De Hope,* and *De Wachter,* among other publications, crystallized in print the community's penchant for scrutinizing itself. Together with gossip and news of the world, they provided a running commentary, often along party lines, on being Dutch in America.

Since 1920 the city of Holland has held a Tulip Festival, which in the latter part of the twentieth century grew to be the third-largest festival in the country. It is, according to its organizers, surpassed only by the

Figure 5. Van Raalte Avenue School, 1908. Courtesy of the Holland Museum Collection at the Joint Archives of Holland.

Tournament of Roses and Mardi Gras among American festivals. More than a half million visitors come to Holland each spring, when tulips are in bloom. They are treated to an endless, brilliantly colored tapestry of flowers—more than a million of them—lining the major streets of the city. Hundreds of acres of surrounding countryside are given over to them as well. Children in authentic folk costumes blanket the downtown area, high school bands from across the nation fill the air with their tuneful thumping, political dignitaries and secret service agents participate in street-scrubbing ceremonies, and the city's half-dozen Dutch culture museums find themselves, for ten days or so, crowded to overflowing.

Into the Modern Age

Many young men of Dutch stock fought with the Allies in the First World War, but while the community began to celebrate its ethnic heritage with a large festival, there was also a shadow hanging over it. Several Americans who were farther from their immigrant roots

Figure 6. Child in traditional Dutch costume. Courtesy of the Holland Museum Collection at the Joint Archives of Holland.

(including the governor of Iowa, where a nearly identical set of Dutch towns and villages had grown up in the nineteenth century) grew suspicious of Dutch-language publications and church services, thinking them too nearly German to be patriotic. As in previous struggles, this issue divided itself along denominational lines. The RCA, being more Americanized, did most of its business in English, and supported the Allies vocally. Many members of the CRC, on the other hand, feeling closer to their Netherlandic roots, still smarted at the bitter memories of the Boer War in South Africa, which had pitted the British against the Dutch. A few prominent leaders voiced their distrust of British motives in 1914, but as U.S. interests grew clearer, they became silent.

One man who did not keep silent was Herman Hoeksema, pastor

of a Christian Reformed Church in Holland. Brushing aside the politics of the war, he vocally refused to fly the American flag during church services, on the grounds that it was a corruption of both religion and politics. Denounced as a Bolshevik in the local press, his life was rhetorically threatened.

> "Every churchman," [said the *Michigan Tradesman*,] "who cannot tolerate the sight of the American flag in his church is a fit subject for deportation or the firing squad." [Hoeksema, in turn,] reacted with an interesting display of his own Americanization. He took to carrying a pistol and, walking home one dark night in Holland, actually threatened to use it upon some would-be assailants.[22]

A few years later the feisty Hoeksema led a breakaway group in forming the Protestant Reformed denomination. The passions excited by the war subsided, and during the next two decades most of the church services and publications in the Dutch language, which had aroused wartime suspicions, died along with their audiences.

The purity campaigns of the perennially fragmented but still thriving Dutch Americans took a new turn in the middle years of the twentieth century. A series of faculty purges at Calvin Seminary preoccupied the upper echelons of the CRC, but most of the community joined in a sweeping nationwide discussion of mores. As a consequence of rapid urban and industrial expansion, America had become a nation of city-dwellers nostalgic for the solid values of an earlier generation's farming villages. For residents of the former *kolonie*, matters were even more complicated: they came from a culture that was congenitally suspicious of prosperity (as described by Simon Schama in his 1987 book *The Embarrassment of Riches*), and now they found themselves prospering beyond the most ambitious dreams of their forbears. Like the rest of the country, the Hollanders of Michigan wondered what to do about the uncertainties of modern life. Women's liberation, drinking, gambling, dancing, movies, evolution, Sunday business, birth control: a horde of contemporary ills, from which the community had sheltered itself for years, came rushing in on it, as if a sociopolitical dike had burst somewhere.

A Joke from the 1950s

Why are Christian Reformed couples not allowed to make love standing up? Because it might lead to dancing.

Reactions to these issues tended, once more, to follow denominational lines. Arguments sometimes raged with the ferocity that only a family fight can engender or endure. The RCA, with its assimilationist stance, tried to keep an open mind, discussing the issues with an air of tolerance while suggesting that moderation, rather than proscription, was the key. The speakers and writers of the CRC distrusted progress and equated moderation with moral indifference. Moderation was, in their minds, like tolerance: a sure sign of impurity. They were almost unanimously opposed to the entire list of "evils." In the case of movies, for example, even good films could not in conscience be patronized, because church leaders insisted that they were part of a godless industry. Where dancing—condemned as intrinsically sexual—was concerned, the prohibition was befuddling. Not only were ballroom and barroom dancing frowned upon, but also Dutch folk dancing, a headline entertainment at the Holland Tulip Festival, where troupes of dancers in traditional costume snaked their way along Van Raalte Avenue. Students from the local high schools were invited to join in the act. *Klompen* dancing, highlighted by the rhythmic clunking of wooden shoes on pavement, had no imaginable erotic overtones, yet the Christian schools of Holland refused to participate, from the 1920s, when the festival began, until the mid-1960s. Gradually, as the years passed, some of the community's proscriptions fell by the wayside. Others were warily lifted by official Synodical proclamation (e.g., the ban on movies in 1968, that on dancing in 1977, that on the teaching of evolution in 1991).

The divergent strategies of these two conservative cultures appear, in a superficial way, in the makeup of the faculty at their respective schools. Less than one-quarter of the faculty have Dutch surnames at Hope College in Holland, while the figure is more than two-thirds

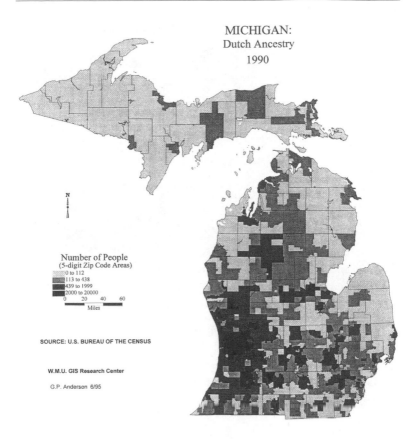

MICHIGAN:
Dutch Ancestry
1990

N

Number of People
(5-digit Zip Code Areas)
0 to 112
113 to 438
439 to 1999
2000 to 20000

0   20   40   60
Miles

SOURCE: U.S. BUREAU OF THE CENSUS

W.M.U. GIS Research Center

G.P. Anderson 6/95

Figure 7. Distribution of Michigan's population claiming Dutch ancestry.

at Calvin College In Grand Rapids. The two communities remain somewhat precariously related to their Dutch heritage and to each other.
The expending of so much energy on parochial issues continues to
reinforce their insularity.

Provisional Conclusions

When historians describe the Dutch communities of Michigan, they are
either scrupulously dispassionate or modestly glowing in their assessments. Neat and amply reasoned documents, well-ordered and comprehensible patterns of development, have an innate appeal to

Figure 8. Windmill Island. Courtesy of the Holland Museum Collection at the Joint Archives of Holland.

historians. Novelists of Dutch descent, writing about the same community, arrive at radically different conclusions, most of them unflattering. In dozens of short stories and novels, Peter De Vries has spent a sizeable portion of his narrative time lampooning the Midwestern Dutch. Especially in *The Blood of the Lamb,* he shows a society with infinite talent for fragmentation along doctrinal lines. The protagonist's father, in fact, sees this tendency as a sign of health: "Rotten wood you can't split," he boasts.

Novelists such as Feike Feikema and David Cornel De Jong emphasize the painful crushing of independent spirits by a narrow, often boorish culture, doom-ridden and bleakly ministerial. The filmmaker Paul Schrader, screenwriter and director of such films as *The Last Temptation of Christ, American Gigolo, Raging Bull,* and *Cat People,* often has

Hollywood in West Michigan

The first ten minutes or so of the 1979 movie Hardcore, which stars George C. Scott, were shot in west Michigan. These opening scenes show, in cinematography reminiscent of Rembrandt, a conservative Dutch family at work and at play. They are lovingly rendered, even though the eventual course of the film does not flatter either the family or the community. I had a nonspeaking part in the movie (singer #1 was my name), and composed some of the soundtrack music. In order to get the necessary permissions, Schrader renamed his film Pilgrim for the span of a week while he was shooting footage in Grand Rapids and environs.

fun with the community in sly visual asides. In *Blue Collar*, for example, Richard Pryor delivers a blisteringly obscene diatribe while wearing a Calvin College sweatshirt. In *Hardcore*, Schrader shows an American Hollander so obsessed with prayer and purity that both his wife and his daughter leave him, the latter for life as a porn princess in California.

Historians and artists thus perceive the community in vastly different ways. The nature and purpose of a well-organized society is to promote group survival, not to nurture individual talent. This quality is what historians—who are, after all, students and employees of the cultural institutions they assess—frequently seek and admire. Artists, on the other hand, approach society from the bottom up, often finding their identity in the delicious freedom to revolt and rebel.

The artists, despite the fact that they constitute only the tiniest segment of a community, suggest the possibility of a third immigrant strategy for coping with American society: to withdraw from the ethnic community, maintaining a certain distance from it without exactly losing touch. Population figures suggest that this third strategy may be employed by the majority: Dutch descendants in the United States number about four million, while ethnic membership in the RCA and the CRC combined amounts to approximately half a million. Seven-eighths of Dutch Americans nationally (a slightly smaller proportion in

Figure 8. Children in Dutch costume. Courtesy of Larry ten Harmsel.

Michigan) are, in the words of one ethnic historian, "lost to the enduring community." Such a phrase reeks mildly of the nineteenth-century
Seceders' language. One is not quite sure what the writer means by "the
enduring community," but such people are not in any sense "lost" to
the larger society, where they add a Netherlandic leavening to businesses, neighborhoods, schools, churches, and the various other cultural institutions in which they find themselves.

The Dutch Triangle is a bulging isosceles wedge of land, with Grand
Rapids at its eastern apex and the lakeside cities of Grand Haven and
Saugatuck at the north and south of its western edge. This region, with
Holland at its historical if not geographic heart, is home to more than
half of Michigan's Dutch American population, estimated at 450,000. It
is a consistently prosperous area, with high rates of employment and
home ownership, vigorous businesses, low rates of crime, virtually
guaranteed election for Republicans at every level of government, reliable municipal services, and excellent school systems. Seen from the
Gerald R. Ford Freeway, which cuts through the middle of the Triangle,

Common Dutch Words

A list of Dutch words still recognized by more than 90 percent of both nursing home residents and high school students surveyed in Holland, Michigan, in the early 1980s:

- *klompen* is preferred by almost everyone over the English terms "clogs" or "wooden shoes";
- *vies*, meaning something worse than "filthy," and often pronounced with a shudder, can serve as adjective, adverb, verb, or noun;
- *kletz*, cognate of the German *Klatsch*, is used mostly in conjunction with the word "coffee," whose English pronunciation is nearly identical to the Dutch;
- *dominee*, minister or pastor
- *vrouw*, woman or wife

Words recognized by 25 to 50 percent of both groups:
- *kerk*, church
- *oma*, grandma
- *opa*, grandpa
- *donder en bliksem*, thunder and lightning
- *Gouda kaas*, cheese from the city of Gouda
- *amandelbroodjes*, a Dutch variety of almond stick
- *boerenjongen*, a form of raisin brandy
- and a variety of barnyard vulgarities not always clearly understood by the speakers.

it looks much like any rural slice of the Midwest, rich in black loam, rolling fields, neat farms, and leafy villages.

The trucks that thunder down the road display many Dutch names—Van Eerden Produce, Heidema Brothers, J. Mollema and Sons, John A. Vanden Bosch, Huizinga Redi-Mix, Talsma Furniture, Wynalda Litho, Dykema Excavators, Herman Miller, and the ubiquitous Meijer. They get washed more often than most semis, appropriately enough,

and display their logos brightly, but they are otherwise indistinguish-
able from trucks anywhere in America. The signs and symbolic struc-
tures visible from the highway show a predilection for windmills, tulips,
and wooden shoes, and occasionally there's a billboard saying something like *Welkom Vrienden.* The language may be a bit foreign, but the
message is clear.

When one leaves the highway for the side roads, the sense of for-
eignness increases. It becomes more apparent that this is a persistent
lump in the American melting pot, a culture that has not merged
entirely with the mainstream. The pristine villages that dot the region,
carefully spaced as if they were distillations of the surrounding farms,
have kept their old-country names: Zutphen, Noordeloos, Borculo,
Graafschap, Bentheim, Drenthe, or Zeeland. In these towns, where on
Sunday nothing is bought or sold and the sound of lawnmowers is
nowhere to be heard, where taverns and movie theaters have never
stood, life strolls along to the peaceful rhythms of the seasons and the
church bells. On a bright day, with puffs of cumulus sliding across the
sky in careful ranks and the white steeples (two apiece for the villages,
dozens in the cities) winking on and off as shade alternates with sun-
light, the viewer could easily imagine that this is a reincarnation—
canals, cows, trees, and all—of the Holland one sees in the rural
paintings of Paulus Potter or the sun-shot landscapes of Hobbema, the
van Ruisdaels, or Rembrandt. It's not, of course. The illusion passes
with the sound of distant traffic. Yet the Dutch Triangle remains a vital,
prosperous, sometimes maddening, sometimes archaic, always vigorous part of Michigan's life.

Dutch Recipes

Boerenjongens *Served during the Christmas season.*

1 lb. raisins
2 cups water
1 cinnamon stick

2 cups sugar
2 cups brandy

Cook raisins, water, and cinnamon about 20 minutes. Add sugar and brandy and cook until dissolved. Fill sterilized container with the mixture. Seal tightly. Let stand three months. Makes 1¾ quarts.

Advocaat *Served during the winter holidays.*

6 eggs
2 Tbsp. sugar

1 quart milk
1 cup brandy

Add ingredients in order and beat until blended. Serves 12.

Appelflappen *A winter treat.*

5 apples
1 Tbsp. vegetable oil

1 cup sugar
1 tsp. salt

2 eggs	2 cups milk
1 cup beer	1 cup flour

Peel and core apples, and slice thinly to make doughnut shapes. Mix and beat other ingredients for batter. Dip apple slices in batter and deep fry in vegetable oil until golden brown. Allow to cool on paper towels. Sprinkle with a 4:1 mixture of sugar and cinnamon. Serves 10–12.

Vetbollen *Dutch fritters.*

1 cup sugar	4 tsp. baking powder
1 Tbsp. shortening	1 tsp. salt
2 eggs	1 cup raisins
2 cups milk	1 large apple, sliced thin
4 cups flour	¼ tsp. nutmeg

Mix ingredients in order. Spoon dollops into hot oil. Deep fry as with doughnuts.

Pannekoeken *Dutch pancakes.*

12 eggs	1 tsp. salt
1 quart milk	1 cup flour

Beat eggs to a froth, add milk and salt. Slowly stirring, add flour. Cook very thin layers in small buttered fry pan. Roll up with butter and brown sugar, chocolate sprinkles, jam, or whatever other sweet thing is at hand.

Louis Padnos

ouis Padnos, a Russian Jewish immigrant who arrived in America near the end of the 19th century, settled in Holland, Michigan, at least partly because of its Netherlandic character. His early history is not documented in traditional historical fashion but survives, like that of most immigrants, because of stories he told his friends and family in later years, and because of tales his family heard—much later—from Russian relatives. Padnos's experience probably resembles, in its uncertainties as well as its determination, that of many young men who came to America in his era.

He left his family in Russia, either because of fears about military conscription, or because of a desire to strike out and find a new life for himself. In any case the young Padnos (he was unsure of his age, but reckoned he was about fourteen or fifteen at this time) made his way to Rotterdam, intending to sail from there to New York. He had no money to pay for his passage, so he spent some time working in Rotterdam, where he found the Dutch language to be close enough to Yiddish that he was able, after a while, to speak it reasonably well.

Once he had saved enough money—it probably took a bit less than a year—he booked passage on a ship sailing from Rotterdam to New York. Upon arrival at Ellis Island, however, he discovered that children of his age were not allowed to enter the country unaccompanied. He found a family of Russian Jews who took him in, and for a few days he posed as one of their sons, getting himself admitted to the country, then heading west as soon as possible. He had heard that the railroads were building—and hiring—in South Dakota.

Padnos's farm family in Russia had been involved in the timber trade on a few occasions, and during his childhood he had learned the Russian techniques for breaking horses. Railroad construction in the Dakotas used teams of horses for much of their heavy hauling, and there was a constant supply of new wild horses that needed to be broken to harness. Padnos was apparently quite good at training these animals, and before long he began buying a few wild horses for himself, breaking them, and selling them independently. After his time in South Dakota, he was able to speak Russian, Yiddish, Dutch, and English. Where language is concerned, the immigrant experience is especially striking: Padnos had skill, fortitude, and the ability to speak four languages, but his economic life remained marginal and uncertain.

After a year or so in the West, he decided he should go to Chicago, where an older married sister of his lived, whom he had not seen since she had left Russia years before. He was able to find her quickly, by the serendipity so often mentioned in immigrant stories: a streetcar conductor, speaking to him in Yiddish, asked him what he was looking for. Padnos related a bit of his recent past, and said he was trying to locate his sister. The conductor told him about a woman who helped newcomers find their way in Chicago, and wrote down her name and address for him. It was her married name he read on the slip of paper.

Because of his facility in Dutch, Padnos was advised by one of his sister's acquaintances to go to west Michigan, where he could deal with people who spoke Dutch. He was supplied with a variety of merchandise for trading, and he soon became an itinerant peddler, plying the small but growing communities in the Dutch Triangle to sell and trade his wares. His partner in Chicago encouraged him to get as many animal pelts as possible, for sale on the East Coast. Hunting and trapping were still at that time common in Michigan, and the fur trade which had spurred the earliest European contacts with the region, although shrunken to smaller proportions, continued to prosper.

Padnos, however, found himself more attracted to the business of recycling scrap metal, and after a couple of years as an itinerant merchant, he settled permanently in Holland, Michigan. There, in 1905, he founded a company, Louis Padnos Iron and Metal, through which his descendants carry on his business—much expanded, refined, and redefined, but still recognizable. At the time he established his business, he was twenty or twenty-one years old.

Logging

When A. C. van Raalte chose to lead his group of immigrants to west Michigan, he knew they would encounter something new to them: dense forests. Van Raalte had opportunities to settle elsewhere. Wisconsin and Iowa were two other states that beckoned. Wisconsin held sizeable existing settlements of Netherlanders, and would have been in many respects an easier place to settle. Iowa, too, offered inducements, especially in large tracts of prairie that needed nothing more than a plow to become farmland. Instead of going to either of these places, however, he consciously chose a site sure to present difficult challenges as it was developed. He spent several weeks in late 1846 and early 1847 exploring northern Allegan and southern Ottawa counties on foot, accompanied by the Reverend Ova Hoyt of Kalamazoo and Judge John Kellogg of Allegan. They endured the severe privations of swamp and woodland in the depths of a Michigan winter, with howling winds and deep snowdrifts; yet van Raalte came out of the experience convinced that this was the place for him and his people.

Some of his reasons for the choice may have been idiosyncratic. He seems to have felt a sense of competition with the Seceder pastor who led a group of immigrants to Iowa, for instance, and Wisconsin was, in his view, too strongly influenced by Dutch Catholics. He wanted a place where relative isolation would allow for the growth of a cohesive religious community. But his strongest reasons for choosing the site now named Holland were eminently sound from an economic standpoint.

He was attracted by the possibility of a shipping harbor on Lake Macatawa (called Black Lake in those days), whose dark waters carried silt from fertile black soil throughout the watershed. He accurately calculated that such fertility could support very intensive farming, and although he was wrong about the harbor—it would be a half century before a reliable shipping channel was constructed—he was absolutely right about the farming.

He was also attracted, rather than put off, by the forests that would have to be cleared before farms, much less towns and cities, could be developed. In fact, van Raalte was so confident he had made the right choice that before the end of January, 1847, he made his first purchase of land in the area, paying $2.15 in delinquent taxes on a 160-acre parcel which he eventually came to own. For the 240 acres that was to form the heart of the future city of Holland he paid $1.25 an acre. Over the next two years he purchased thousands of surrounding acres at per-acre prices ranging from 75¢ to $5.00. This land, which he sold to settlers, provided him with an income and a modicum of wealth for the rest of his life. His commitment to this particular landscape (discussed in detail by Robert P. Swierenga in his article "Decisions, Decisions: Turning Points in the Founding of Holland," *Michigan Historical Review*, Spring 1998, pp. 49-72) was both Calvinistic and pragmatic.

First, the forests would provide honest, productive work for people who had lived with poverty and unemployment in the Netherlands (one of God's first commandments to Adam: "in the sweat of thy brow shalt thou earn thy bread"). The minute a tree was felled, a garden could be planted. Logs could be used for building shelter, they could be sold for cash, they could help establish a point of connection between the tiny budding economy of the settlers and the more well-established institutions of the burgeoning American Midwest. Sawmills and other small industrial establishments were sure to arise where there was timber to be had, and once the land was cleared farms would emerge, providing a solid economic basis for life well into the future.

The immigrants had no experience with logging—something their native land was never noted for. They suffered some injuries and deaths from falling timber in their first attempts to clear land. But eventually they learned to do it well. Michigan was in the early stages of a lumbering boom which created immense fortunes, which filled the springtime rivers of the state with logs, which established nearby Grand Rapids as the furniture capital of the United States, which spawned a host of subsidiary enterprises, and which, by the end of the nineteenth century, left the state virtually denuded.

The white pine forests of the north, together with the oak and maple stands farther south had been stripped. The state was scarred from north to south and from east to west. Its major natural resource, thought by some to be inexhaustible, was gone. However, from the standpoint of the settlers, Michigan's lumbering excesses were a stroke of luck. Without compromising their own society and its ideals, they were able to develop products and talents and businesses that gave them a significant foothold in the New World. Van Raalte's decision to cast his lot in a neglected corner of Michigan paid dividends on many fronts. In the second half of the nineteenth century, the Dutch Triangle was able to put together a multi-faceted, integrated economy strong enough to survive even the ravages of the Depression.

Streetscape, Holland, Michigan. Photo by Earl W. Rutz.

Notes

1. Robert P. Swierenga, "The Dutch Transplanting in Michigan and the Midwest," the Clarence M. Burton Memorial Lecture, Historical Society of Michigan, 1985, 2.
2. Anthonie Brummelkamp and Albertus C. Van Raalte, *Landverhuizing* (Amsterdam. privately printed, 1846), 3.
3. Ibid., 6.
4. Ibid., 8.
5. Stephen Henry Lucas, *Netherlanders in America* (Grand Rapids, Mich.: William B. Eerdmans Publishing Company, 1989), 94.
6. Ibid.
7. Herbert Brinks, *Write Back Soon: Letters from Immigrants in America* (Grand Rapids, Mich.: William B. Eerdmans Publishing Company, 1986), 36.
8. Henry S. Lucas, whose magisterial *Netherlanders in America* teems with individual case histories, left his papers to the Bentley Historical Library in Ann Arbor, where some of the anecdotal materials in this essay were gleaned.
9. Helen Hornbeck Tanner, ed. *Atlas of Great Lakes Indians* (Norman, Ok.: University of Oklahoma Press, 1987), 169–74.
10. Simon Schama, *The Embarrassment of Riches* (New York: Knopf, 1987), 266.
11. Herbert Brinks, Curator of the Heritage Hall archives at Calvin College, has **39**

gathered, translated, and published many immigrant letters in *Write Back Soon* and a forthcoming book still in press. As editor of *Origins,* he has overseen the resurrection of many documents relating to the Dutch community—especially the Christian Reformed Church—throughout North America.

12. Robert P. Swierenga, at Kent State University, has compiled the most useful and exhaustive statistical studies of Dutch immigration patterns. Most of the data-based information in this essay comes from his work, either directly or indirectly in the form of assistance provided by his former student Larry J. Wagenaar, former archivist of the Joint Archives of the Holland Historical Trust, and now head of the Historical Society of Michigan.

13. *Minutes of Classis Holland,* A.D. *1848–1858* (Grand Rapids, Mich.: Christian Reformed Publishing House, 1950), 179.

14. Brinks, 1986, 54.

15. *Minutes,* 125.

16. Ibid., 240.

17. William Van Eyck, *Landmarks of the Reformed Fathers* (Grand Rapids, Mich.: Reformed Press, 1922), 34.

18. James H. Bratt's *Dutch Calvinism in Modern America,* a witty and perceptive history of ideas, delineates the split between the RCA and the CRC, together with various purity campaigns, in numbing detail. The book also offers a thorough, intelligent assessment of the work of four Dutch-American novelists.

19. Herbert Brinks, "Civil War: Dutch American Reactions," *Origins* 6, no. 1 (1988): 13.

20. Hendrik G. Meijer, *Thrifty Years: The Life of Hendrik Meijer* (Grand Rapids, Mich.: William B. Eerdmans Publishing Company, 1984), 53–54.

21. Ibid., 37.

22. James H. Bratt, *Dutch Calvinism in Modern America: A History of a Conservative Subculture* (Grand Rapids, Mich.: William B. Eerdmans Publishing Company, 1984), 89.

Dutch heritage, Holland, Michigan. Photo by Earl W. Rutz.

For Further Reference

An asterisk indicates those works especially beneficial for readers who would like to learn more about the Dutch in America.

General

Anonymous (initialed M.G. in what claims to be the author's signature). "De landverhuizing naar de Vereenigte Staaten" ("Emigration to the United States"). *Bergen op zoom,* the Netherlands: privately printed, 1853.

Bakker, M. J.. "Letter." Ann Arbor: Bentley Historical Library. February 1872.

Bjorklund, Elaine M. "Ideology and Culture Exemplified in Southwestern Michigan," *Annals of the Association of American Geographers* 54, no. 2 (June 1964): 227–41.

Blouin, Francis X, Jr., and Robert M. Warner. *Sources for the Study of Migration and Ethnicity.* Ann Arbor: University of Michigan Press, 1979.

*Bratt, James H. *Dutch Calvinism in Modern America: A History of a Conservative Subculture.* Grand Rapids, Mich.: William B. Eerdmans Publishing Company, 1984.

*Brinks, Herbert. "Recent Dutch Immigration to the United States," In *Continental American Immigration,* edited by Dennis Lawrence Cuddy, 137–54. Boston: Twayne, 1982.

———. *Write Back Soon: Letters from Immigrants in America.* Grand Rapids, Mich.: William B. Eerdmans Publishing Company, 1986.

———, comp. *Immigration Sources Project (Netherlands).* Ann Arbor, Mich.: Bentley Historical Library, n. d..

————. "Civil War: Dutch American Reactions," *Origins* 6, no. 1(1988): 21.

Brummelkamp, A., and A. C. Van Raalte. *Landverhuizing*. Amsterdam: privately printed, 1846.

Clifton, James H. *The Pokagons, 1683–1983: Catholic Potawatamie Indians of the St. Joseph River Valley*. Lanham, Md.: University Press of America, 1984.

*De Jong, Gerald F. *The Dutch in America 1609–1974*. Boston: Twayne, 1975.

Huizinga, J. H. *Dutch Civilization in the Seventeenth Century and Other Essays*. New York: Harper & Row, 1968. (Translation of essays first published in the 1930s).

Holland Junior Welfare League, eds. *Eet Smakkelijk: Official Cookbook of Holland, Michigan*. Holland, Mich.: Steketee-Van Huis, 1964.***

*Lucas, Henry Stephen. *Netherlanders in America*. Ann Arbor: University of Michigan Press, 1955. Reprint, Grand Rapids, Mich.: William B. Eerdmans Publishing Company, 1989.

May, George, and Herbert Brinks. *A Michigan Reader: 11,000 B.C. to A.D. 1865*. Grand Rapids, Mich.: William B. Eerdmans Publishing Company, 1974.

Meijer, Hendrik G. *Thrifty Years: The Life of Hendrik Meijer*. Grand Rapids, Mich.: William B. Eerdmans Publishing Company, 1984.

Minutes of Classis Holland, A.D. 1848–1858. Grand Rapids, Mich.: Christian Reformed Publishing House, 1950.

Mulder, Arnold. "Americans from Holland." *The Peoples of America Series*, ed. Louis Adamic. Philadelphia: Lippencott, 1947.

Schama, Simon. *The Embarrassment of Riches*. New York: Knopf, 1987.

Swierenga, Robert P. "Dutch." In *Harvard Encyclopedia of American Ethnic Groups*. Cambridge: The Belknap Press of Harvard University, 1980.

————, comp. *Dutch Immigrants in U.S. Ship Passenger Manifests, 1820–1880: An Alphabetical Listing by Household and Independent Persons*. Wilmington, Del.: Scholarly Resources, 1983.

————. "The Dutch Transplanting in Michigan and the Midwest." The Clarence M. Burton Memorial Lecture, Historical Society of Michigan, 1985.

Tanner, Helen Hornbeck, ed. "Epidemics," In *Atlas of Great Lakes Indian History*, 169–74. Norman, Ok.: University of Oklahoma Press, 1987.

ten Harmsel, Johan. "Werkeloosheid" ("Unemployment"). Manuscript essay, Nijverdal, the Netherlands. Private collection, Kalamazoo, 1900.

Ten Harmsel, Larry. "Dutch Language Remnants in Holland, Michigan." In *Journal of Regional Cultures*, 2, no. 2 (1982): 71-77.

————. "Dutch." In *American Immigrant Cultures: Builders of a Nation*. New York: MacMillan, 1997.

Van der Veen, Engbertus. *The Life History and Reminiscences of Engbertus Van der Veen*. Holland, Mich.: Steletee-Van Huis, 1911.

Van Eyck, William. *Landmarks of the Reformed Fathers*. Grand Rapids, Mich.: Reformed Press, 1922.

*van Hinte, Jacob. *Netherlands in America: A Study of Emigration and Settlement in the United States of America*. Grand Rapids, Mich.: Baker Books, 1985. (Republication of 1928 edition in Dutch: translated by A. De Wit; general editor, Robert P. Swierenga).

Fiction

*Brashler, William. *The Chosen Prey*. New York: Harper & Row, 1985.

De Jong, David Cornel. *Belly Fulla Straw*. New York: Houghton Mifflin, 1943.

————. *With a Dutch Accent*. New York: Houghton Mifflin, 1944.

*De Vries, Peter. *The Blood of the Lamb*. Boston: Little, Brown, 1961.

————. *Without a Stitch in Time*. Boston: Little, Brown, 1972.

Feikema, Feike. *The Primitive*. New York: Houghton Mifflin, 1949.

Keuning, J. *The Man in Bearskin*. Grand Rapids, Mich.: Eerdmans. Publishing Company, 1940 (unacknowledged translation of an earlier novel, *De man in beerenhuid*, 1929).

Lieuwen, John. *Troebel en Fon*. Holland, Mich.: Steketee-Van Huis, 1938.

————. *Sweat en Tears*. Holland, Mich.: Steketee-Van Huis, 1947.

Meeter, Glenn. *Letters to Barbara*. Grand Rapids, Mich.: William B. Eerdmans Publishing Company, 1981.

Mulder, Arnold. *The Dominie of Harlem*. Chicago: A. C. McClurg, 1913.

————. *Bram of the Five Corners*. Chicago: A. C. McClurg, 1915.

————. *The Outbound Road*. Boston: Houghton Mifflin, 1919.

Nieland, Dirk. *Yankee-Dutch*. Grand Rapids, Mich.: Eerdmans-Sevensma, 1919.

————. *'N Fonnie Bisnis*. Grand Rapids, Mich.: William B. Eerdmans Publishing Company, 1929.

Archives

Although many of the Dutch settlements have local museums and historical societies, the most accessible (and best) collections can be found in these three places.

- The Bentley Historical Library, University of Michigan, Ann Arbor. Francis X. Blouin archivist.
- Heritage Hall, Calvin College, Grand Rapids, Michigan. Herbert J. Brinks, archivist.
- The Joint Archives of Holland, Hope College, Holland, Michigan. Larry J. Wagenaar, archivist.

Index

A

American Indians, 5, 6, 8, 9, 10
Allegan (Mich.), 7, 35

B

Belgic Confessions, 2
Bentham (Mich.), 28
Black Lake, 36
Borculo (Mich.), 28
Brummelkamp, Anthonie, 3, 4, 6

C

Calvin College, 18, 23
Chicago, 32
Christian Reformed Church, 14, 18,
    20, 21, 22, 25
Civil War, 12, 14, 15

D

De Jong, David Cornel, 24
De Vries, Peter, 24
Drenthe (Mich.), 8, 12, 28

E

Ellis Island, 31
Erasmus, 3
Evolution, 21, 22

F

Flags in Church, 21
Feikema, Feike, 24

G

Graafschap (Mich.), 28
Grand Haven (Mich.), 12, 25
Grand Rapids (Mich.), 7, 12, 16, 18,
    25

H

Harlem (Mich.), 8
Hobbema, 28
Hoeksema, Herman, 20, 21
Holland (Mich.), 6, 7, 8, 10, 16, 18, 19,
    21, 25, 31, 33, 36
Hope College, 15, 18, 22

Hoyt, Rev. Ova, 35

I
Iowa, 35

J
Java, 4, 7

K
Kalamazoo (Mich.), 12, 35
Kellogg, John, 35
Kuiper, R. T., 12

L
Lake Macatawa (Black Lake), 36

M
Meijer, Hendrik, 16, 17, 18
Muskegon (Mich.), 12

N
Nieuwenhuis, Domela, 17
Noordeloos (Mich.), 28

O
Overisel (Mich.), 8
Ottawa County (Mich.), 35

P
Padnos, Louis, 31–33
Potatoes, 3, 4, 16
Potter, Paulus, 28
Pryor, Richard, 25

R
Reformed Church in America, 13, 14,
    18, 20, 22, 25
Rembrandt, 3, 25, 28
Rotterdam (Netherlands), 31

S
Schrader, Paul, 24, 25
Scott, George C., 25
Seceders, 2, 3, 4, 5
South Dakota, 32
Spinoza, 3
Swierenga, Robert P., 36

T
Tobacco in Church, 11

V
Van der Veen, Engbertus, 7
Van Gogh, Vincent, 16
van Raalte, Albertus, 2, 4, 6, 8, 10, 15,
    35–37
van Raalte, Dirk, 15
van Ruisdaels, 28
Vriesland (Mich.), 8

W
William I, 2
Wisconsin, 35

Z
Zeeland (Mich.), 28
Zutphen (Mich.), 28